European Country Maps Coloring Book

46 Blank, Outline and Detailed Country Maps for Coloring, Home, and Education

Illustrations by J. Bruce Jones

European Country Maps Coloring Book
46 Blank, Outline and Detailed Country Maps for Coloring, Home, and Education
Concept, creating, editing and illustrations by J. Bruce Jones

© Copyright J. Bruce Jones 2020 All rights reserved.

Original map illustrations by J. Bruce Jones and the World of Maps Collections

Permission for reproduction of this material by the classroom teacher or instructor for use with students or homeschool, not commercial resale, is granted by virtue of purchase of this book. Such permission does not include the storage of any part of this book in a retrieval system or the transmission of such, in any form, or by any means, electronic, mechanical, recording, or other-wise, without prior permission of the author, except as provided by the USA copyright law.

The printable, blank, detailed and outline maps in this coloring book can be freely photocopied by a teacher or parent for use in a classroom or for home lessons.

J. Bruce Jones
Mystic, CT 06355
781-492-0742
www.freeusandworldmaps.com

European Country Maps Coloring Book

© Copyright Bruce Jones Design Inc. 2020
www.mapsfordesign.com

Europe

© Copyright Bruce Jones Design Inc. 2020
www.mapsfordesign.com

Europe

© Copyright Bruce Jones Design Inc. 2020
www.mapsfordesign.com

Europe

© Copyright Bruce Jones Design Inc. 2020
www.mapsfordesign.com

Europe

© Copyright Bruce Jones Design Inc. 2020
www.mapsfordesign.com

Europe Global Projection

© Copyright Bruce Jones Design Inc. 2020
www.mapsfordesign.com

Europe Global Projection

© Copyright Bruce Jones Design Inc. 2020
www.mapsfordesign.com

Albania

© Copyright Bruce Jones Design Inc. 2020
www.mapsfordesign.com

Albania

© Copyright Bruce Jones Design Inc. 2020
www.mapsfordesign.com

Austria

© Copyright Bruce Jones Design Inc. 2020
www.mapsfordesign.com

Austria

© Copyright Bruce Jones Design Inc. 2020
www.mapsfordesign.com

Belarus

© Copyright Bruce Jones Design Inc. 2020
www.mapsfordesign.com

Belarus

© Copyright Bruce Jones Design Inc. 2020
www.mapsfordesign.com

Belgium & Luxembourg

© Copyright Bruce Jones Design Inc. 2020
www.mapsfordesign.com

Belgium & Luxembourg

© Copyright Bruce Jones Design Inc. 2020
www.mapsfordesign.com

Bosnia and Herzegovina

© Copyright Bruce Jones Design Inc. 2020
www.mapsfordesign.com

Bosnia and Herzegovina

© Copyright Bruce Jones Design Inc. 2020
www.mapsfordesign.com

Bulgaria

© Copyright Bruce Jones Design Inc. 2020
www.mapsfordesign.com

Bulgaria

© Copyright Bruce Jones Design Inc. 2020
www.mapsfordesign.com

Croatia

© Copyright Bruce Jones Design Inc. 2020
www.mapsfordesign.com

Croatia

© Copyright Bruce Jones Design Inc. 2020
www.mapsfordesign.com

Cyprus

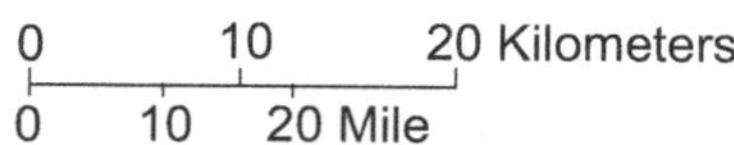

© Copyright Bruce Jones Design Inc. 2020
www.mapsfordesign.com

Cyprus

© Copyright Bruce Jones Design Inc. 2020
www.mapsfordesign.com

Czech Republic

© Copyright Bruce Jones Design Inc. 2020
www.mapsfordesign.com

Czech Republic

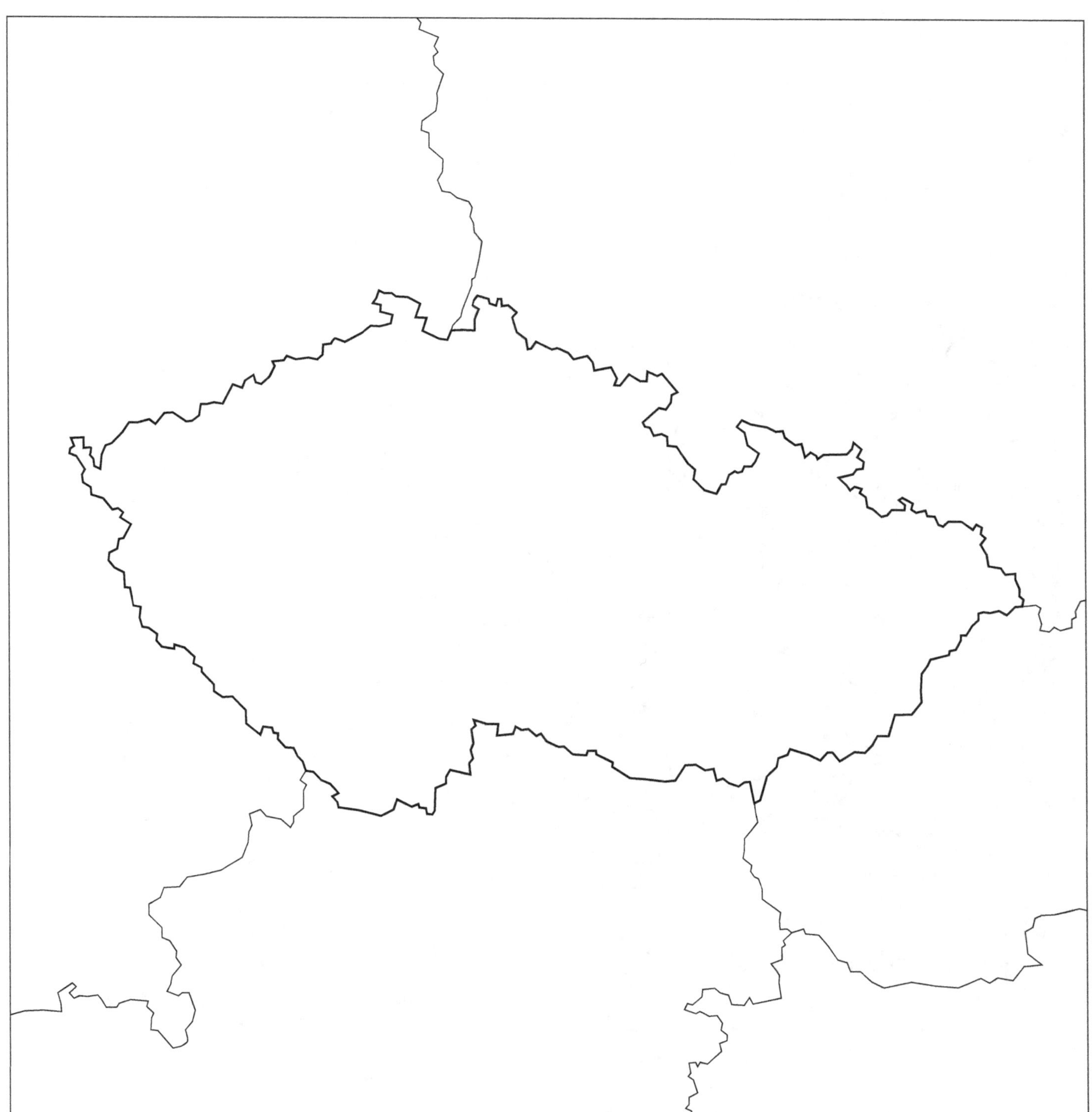

© Copyright Bruce Jones Design Inc. 2020
www.mapsfordesign.com

Denmark

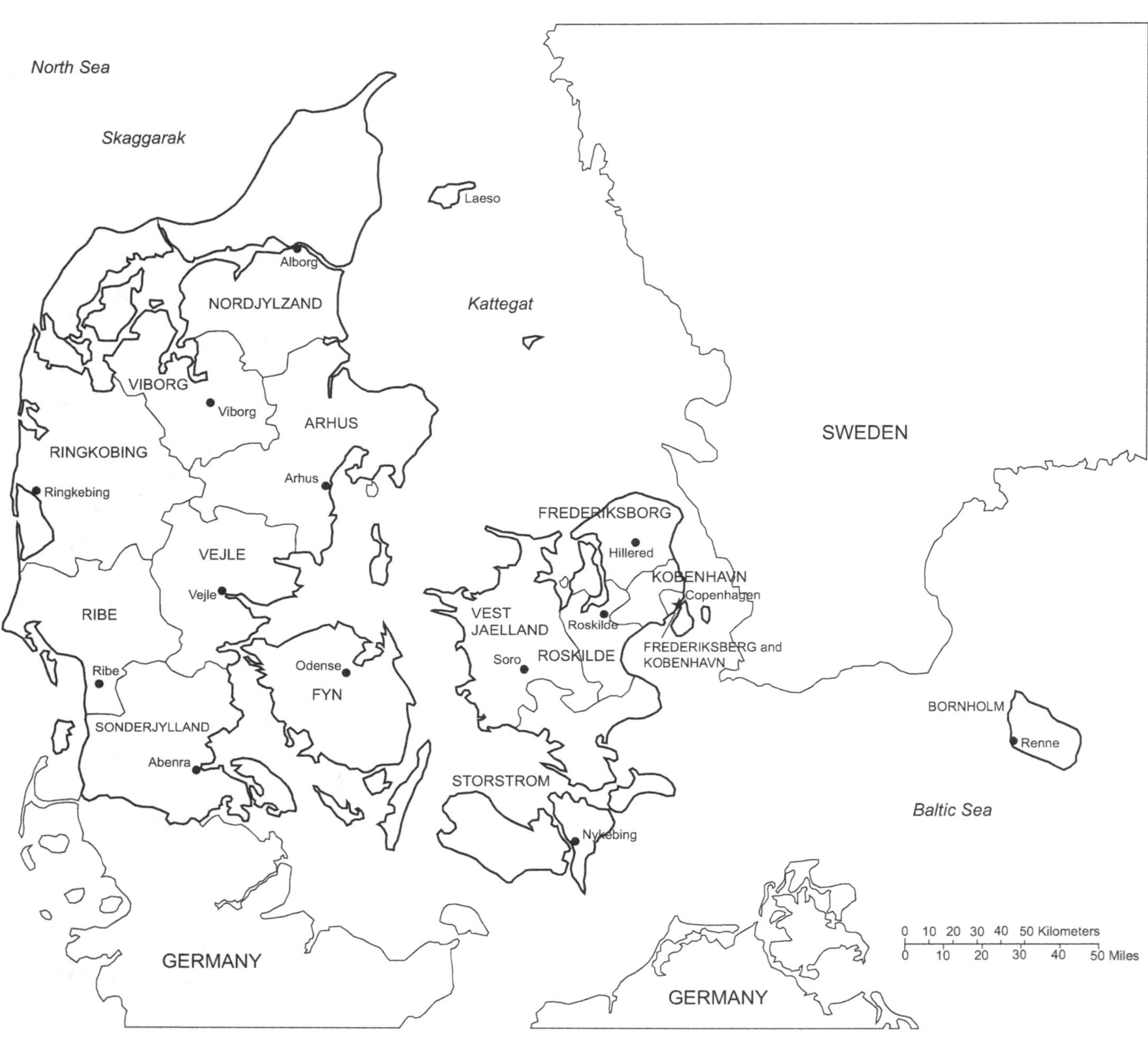

© Copyright Bruce Jones Design Inc. 2020
www.mapsfordesign.com

Denmark

© Copyright Bruce Jones Design Inc. 2020
www.mapsfordesign.com

Estonia

© Copyright Bruce Jones Design Inc. 2020
www.mapsfordesign.com

30

Estonia

© Copyright Bruce Jones Design Inc. 2020
www.mapsfordesign.com

Finland

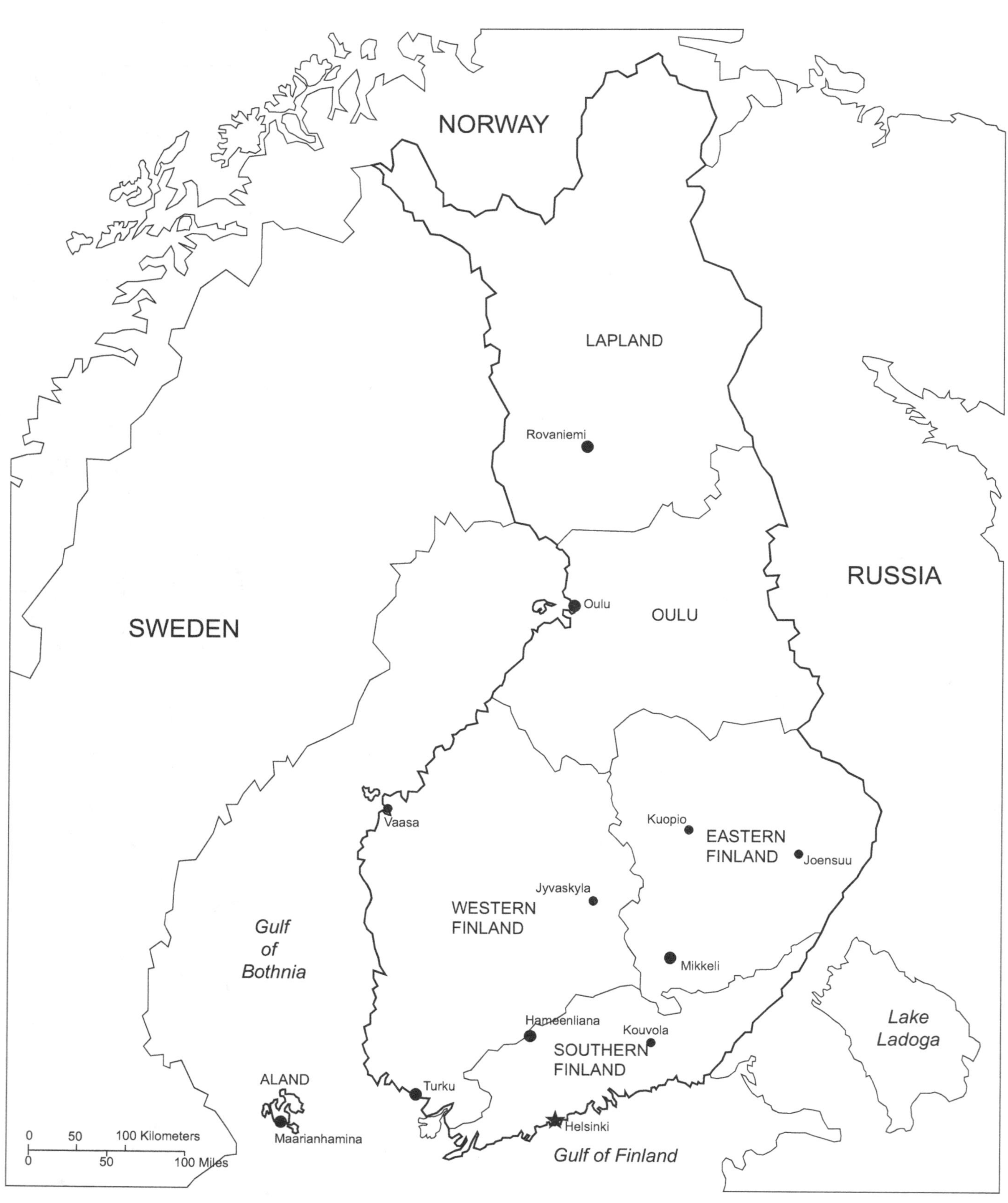

© Copyright Bruce Jones Design Inc. 2020
www.mapsfordesign.com

Finland

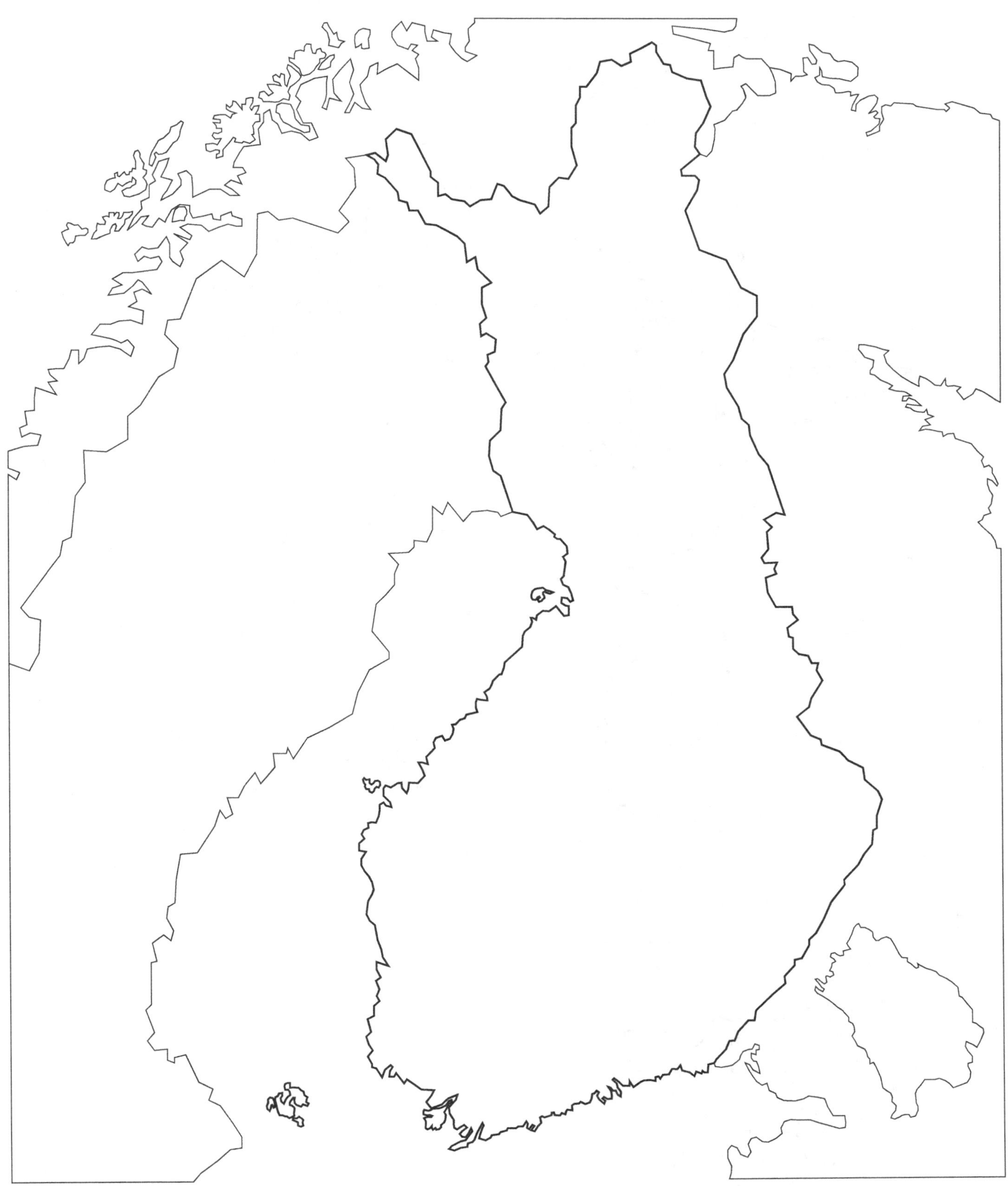

© Copyright Bruce Jones Design Inc. 2020
www.mapsfordesign.com

France

© Copyright Bruce Jones Design Inc. 2020
www.mapsfordesign.com

34

France

© Copyright Bruce Jones Design Inc. 2020
www.mapsfordesign.com

France • Administrative Districts

© Copyright Bruce Jones Design Inc. 2020
www.mapsfordesign.com

36

France • Administrative Districts

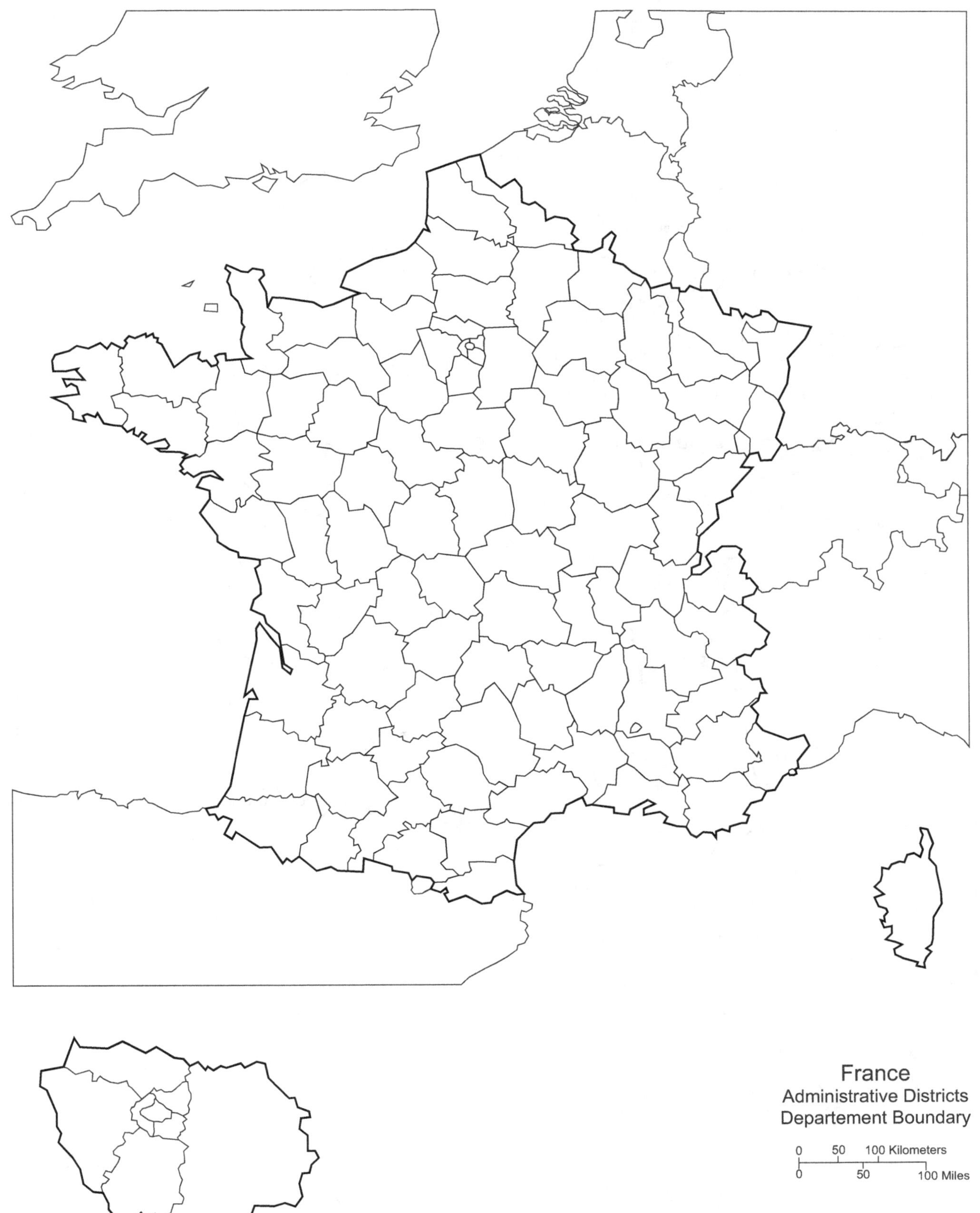

© Copyright Bruce Jones Design Inc. 2020
www.mapsfordesign.com

France • Provincial Boundaries

France
Provincial Boundaries

0 50 100 Kilometers
0 50 100 Miles

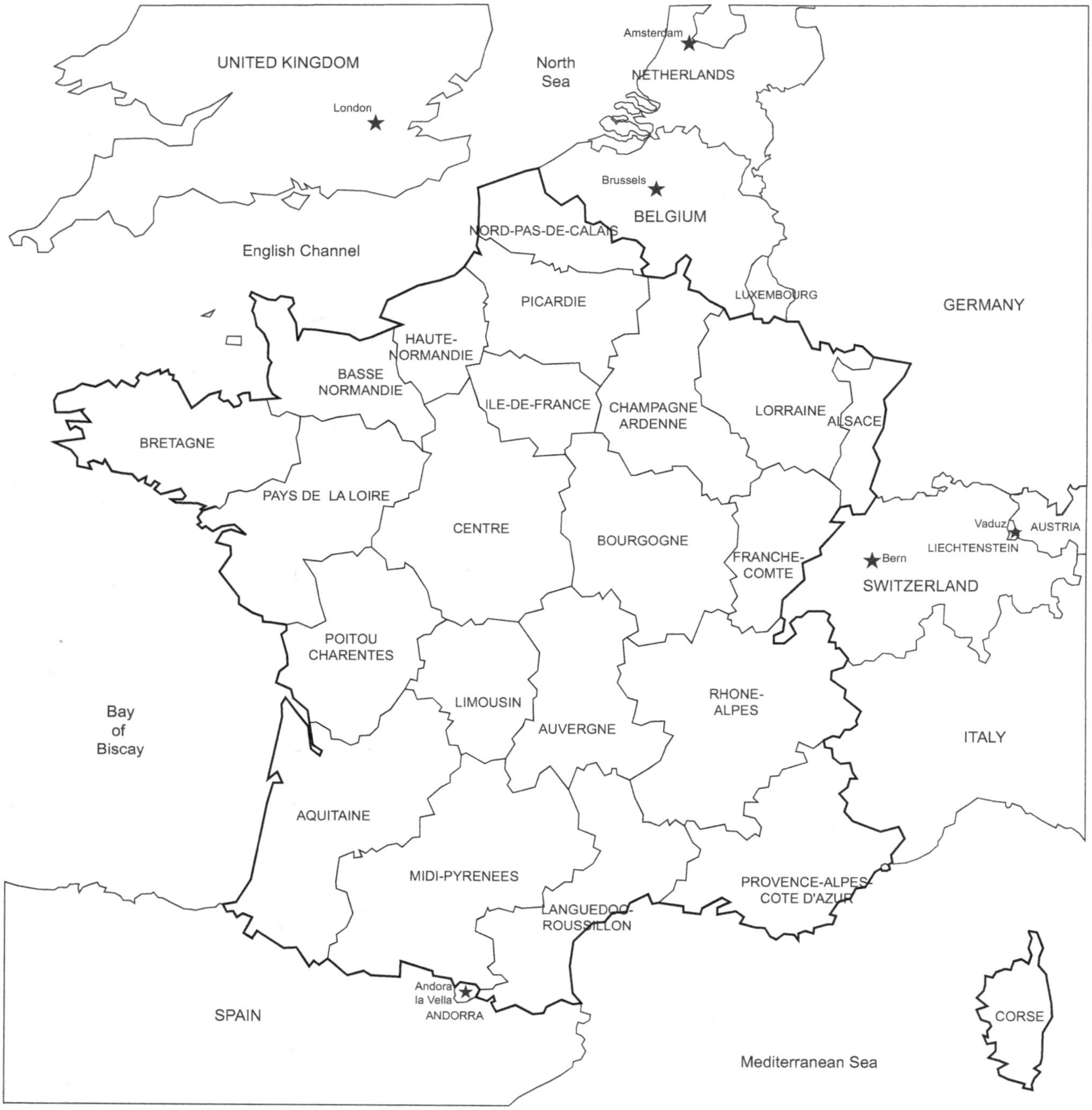

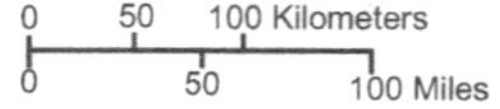

© Copyright Bruce Jones Design Inc. 2020
www.mapsfordesign.com

France • Provincial Boundaries

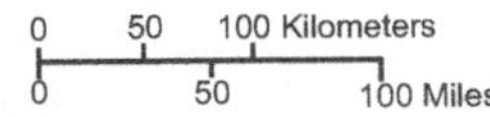

© Copyright Bruce Jones Design Inc. 2020
www.mapsfordesign.com

Germany

© Copyright Bruce Jones Design Inc. 2020
www.mapsfordesign.com

Germany

© Copyright Bruce Jones Design Inc. 2020
www.mapsfordesign.com

Greece

© Copyright Bruce Jones Design Inc. 2020
www.mapsfordesign.com

Greece

© Copyright Bruce Jones Design Inc. 2020
www.mapsfordesign.com

Hungary

© Copyright Bruce Jones Design Inc. 2020
www.mapsfordesign.com

Hungary

© Copyright Bruce Jones Design Inc. 2020
www.mapsfordesign.com

Iceland

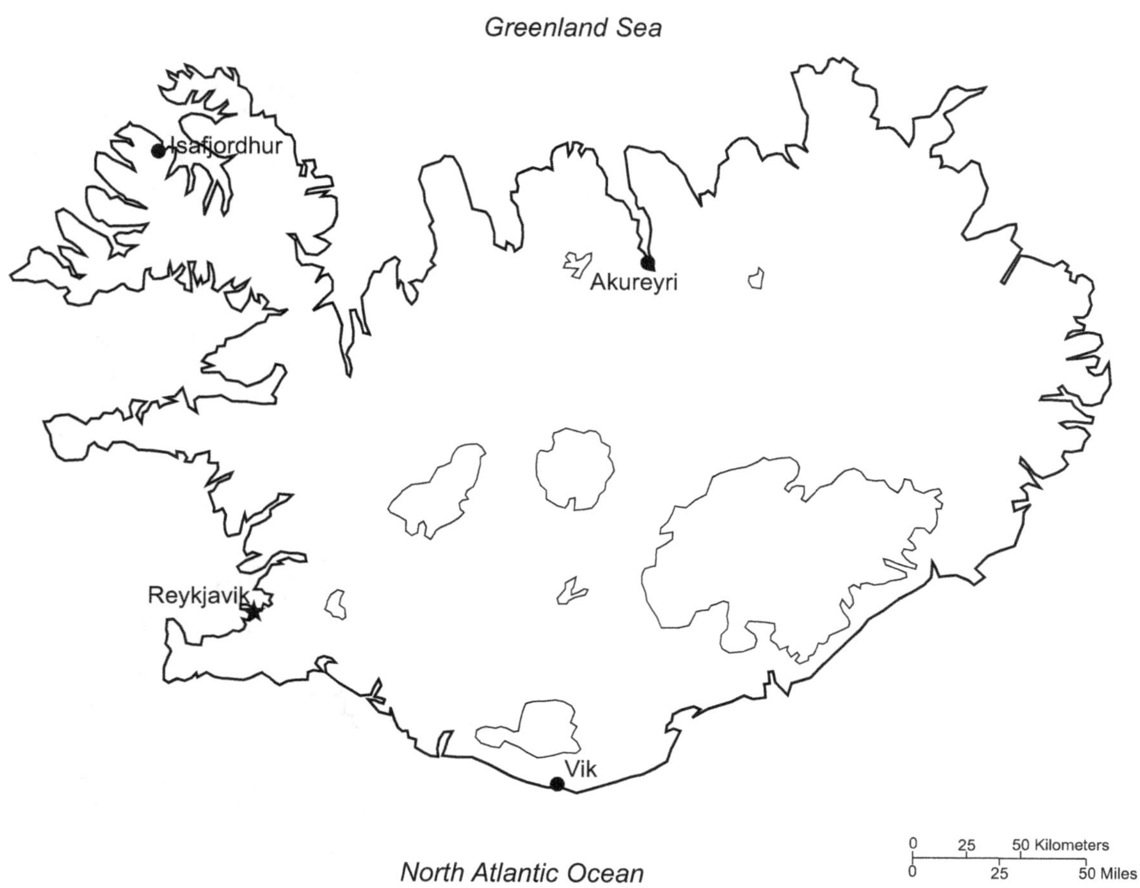

© Copyright Bruce Jones Design Inc. 2020
www.mapsfordesign.com

Iceland

© Copyright Bruce Jones Design Inc. 2020
www.mapsfordesign.com

Ireland

© Copyright Bruce Jones Design Inc. 2020
www.mapsfordesign.com

Ireland

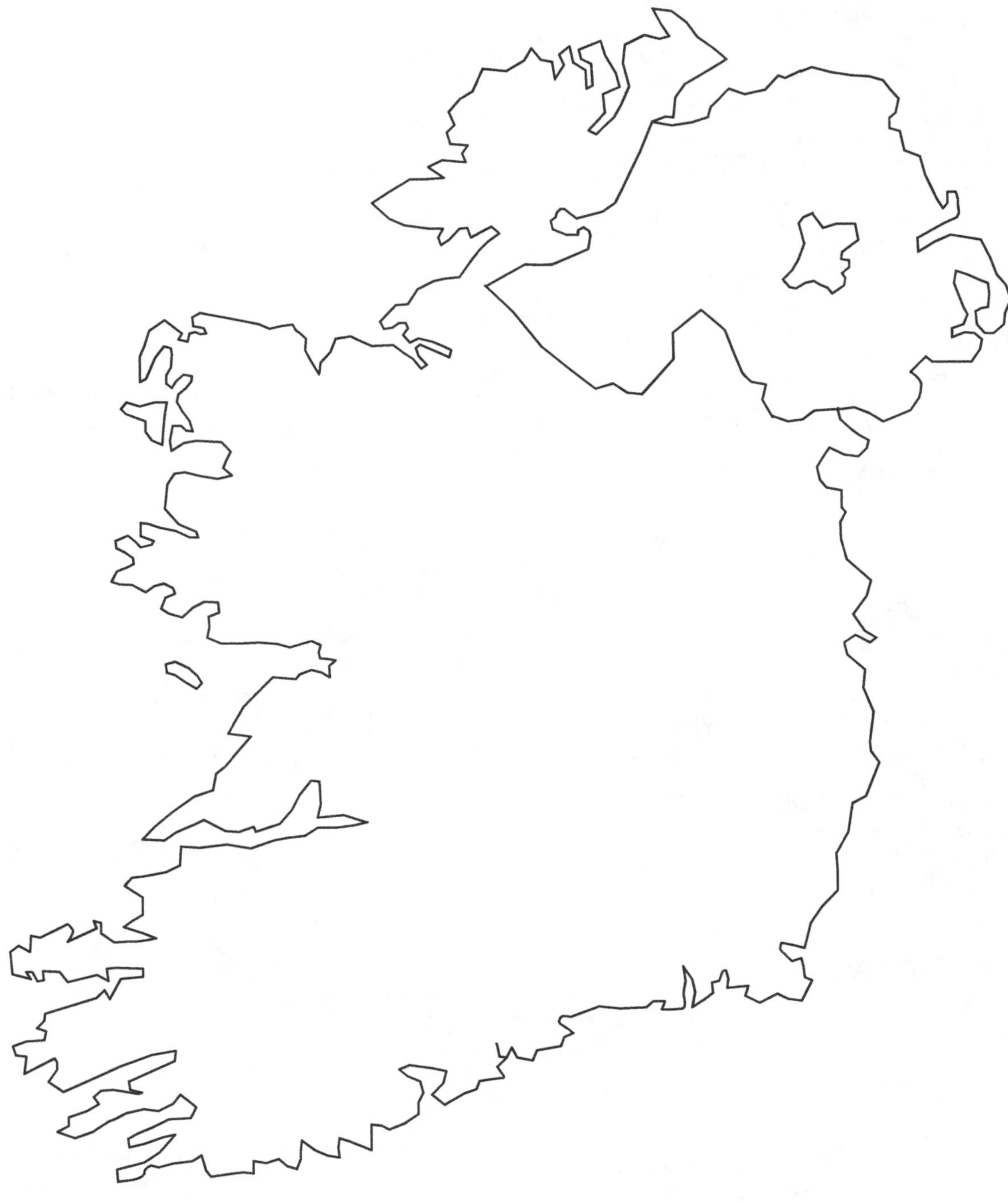

© Copyright Bruce Jones Design Inc. 2020
www.mapsfordesign.com

Italy

© Copyright Bruce Jones Design Inc. 2020
www.mapsfordesign.com

50

Italy

© Copyright Bruce Jones Design Inc. 2020
www.mapsfordesign.com

Kosovo

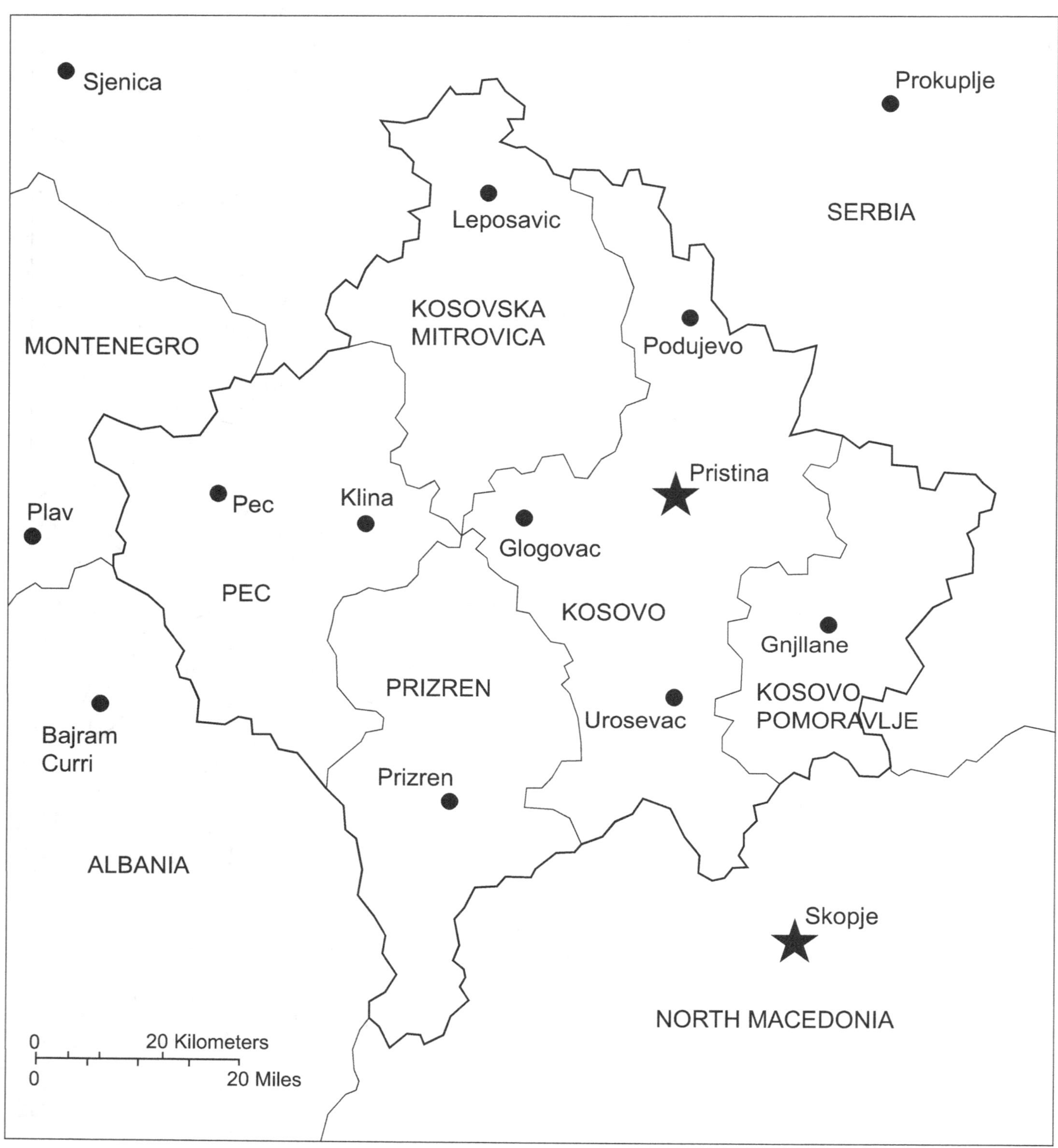

© Copyright Bruce Jones Design Inc. 2020
www.mapsfordesign.com

Kosovo

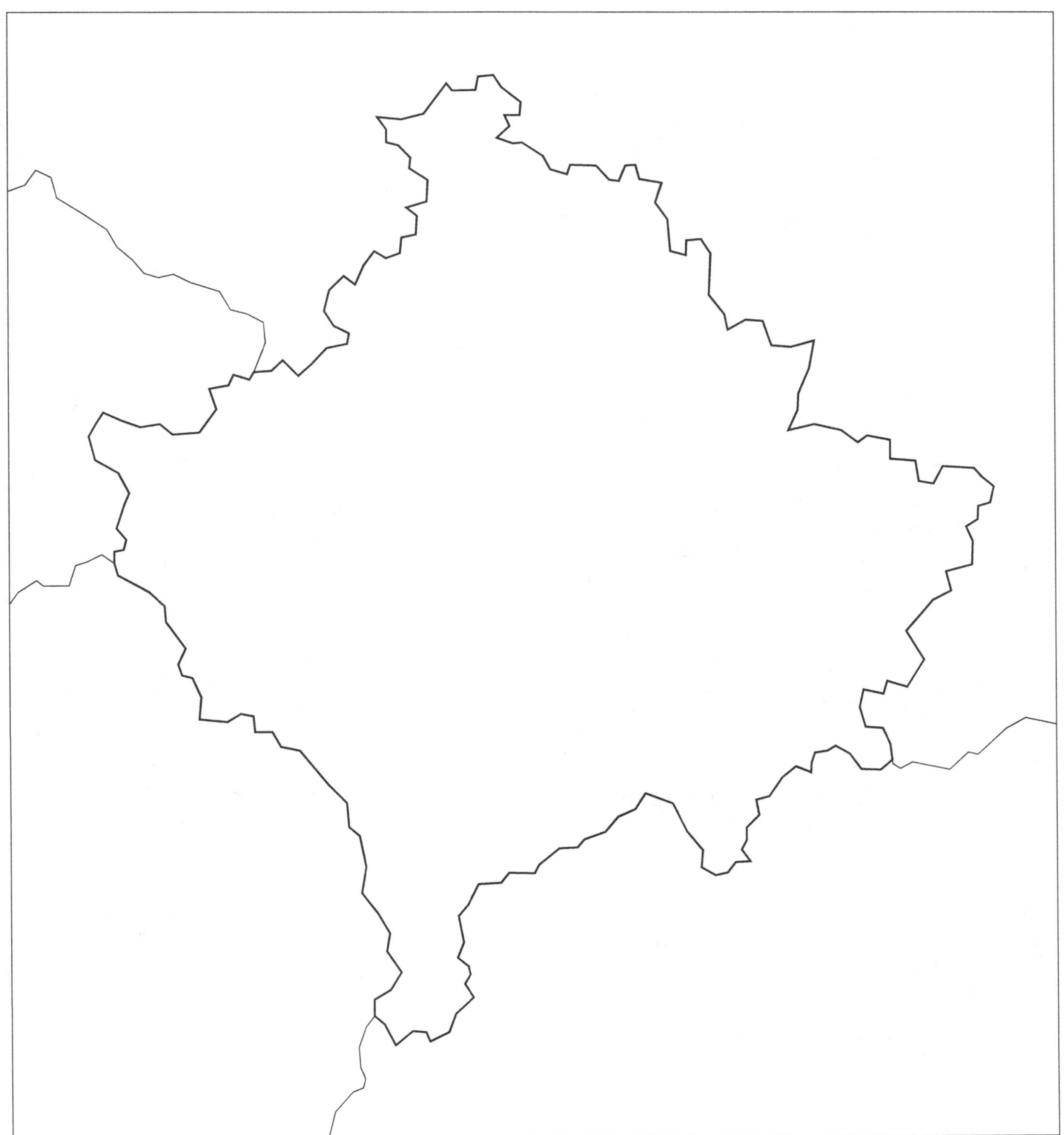

© Copyright Bruce Jones Design Inc. 2020
www.mapsfordesign.com

Latvia

© Copyright Bruce Jones Design Inc. 2020
www.mapsfordesign.com

Lativia

© Copyright Bruce Jones Design Inc. 2020
www.mapsfordesign.com

Lithuania

© Copyright Bruce Jones Design Inc. 2020
www.mapsfordesign.com

Lithuania

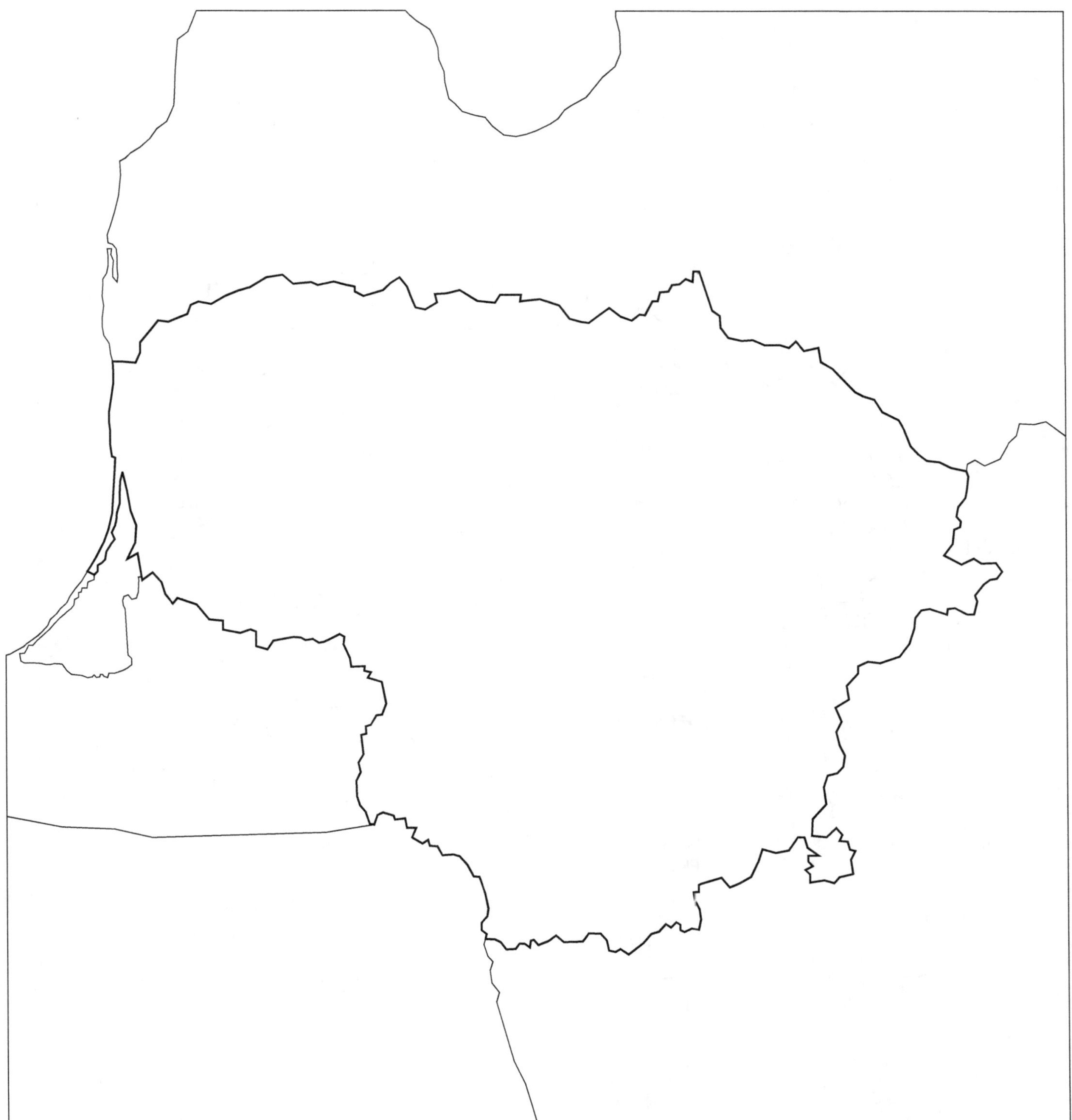

© Copyright Bruce Jones Design Inc. 2020
www.mapsfordesign.com

North Macedonia

© Copyright Bruce Jones Design Inc. 2020
www.mapsfordesign.com

North Macedonia

© Copyright Bruce Jones Design Inc. 2020
www.mapsfordesign.com

59

Malta

© Copyright Bruce Jones Design Inc. 2020
www.mapsfordesign.com

Malta

© Copyright Bruce Jones Design Inc. 2020
www.mapsfordesign.com

Moldova

© Copyright Bruce Jones Design Inc. 2020
www.mapsfordesign.com

Moldova

© Copyright Bruce Jones Design Inc. 2020
www.mapsfordesign.com

Montenegro

© Copyright Bruce Jones Design Inc. 2020
www.mapsfordesign.com

64

Montenegro

© Copyright Bruce Jones Design Inc. 2020
www.mapsfordesign.com

Netherlands

© Copyright Bruce Jones Design Inc. 2020
www.mapsfordesign.com

Netherlands

© Copyright Bruce Jones Design Inc. 2020
www.mapsfordesign.com

Norway

© Copyright Bruce Jones Design Inc. 2020
www.mapsfordesign.com

68

Norway

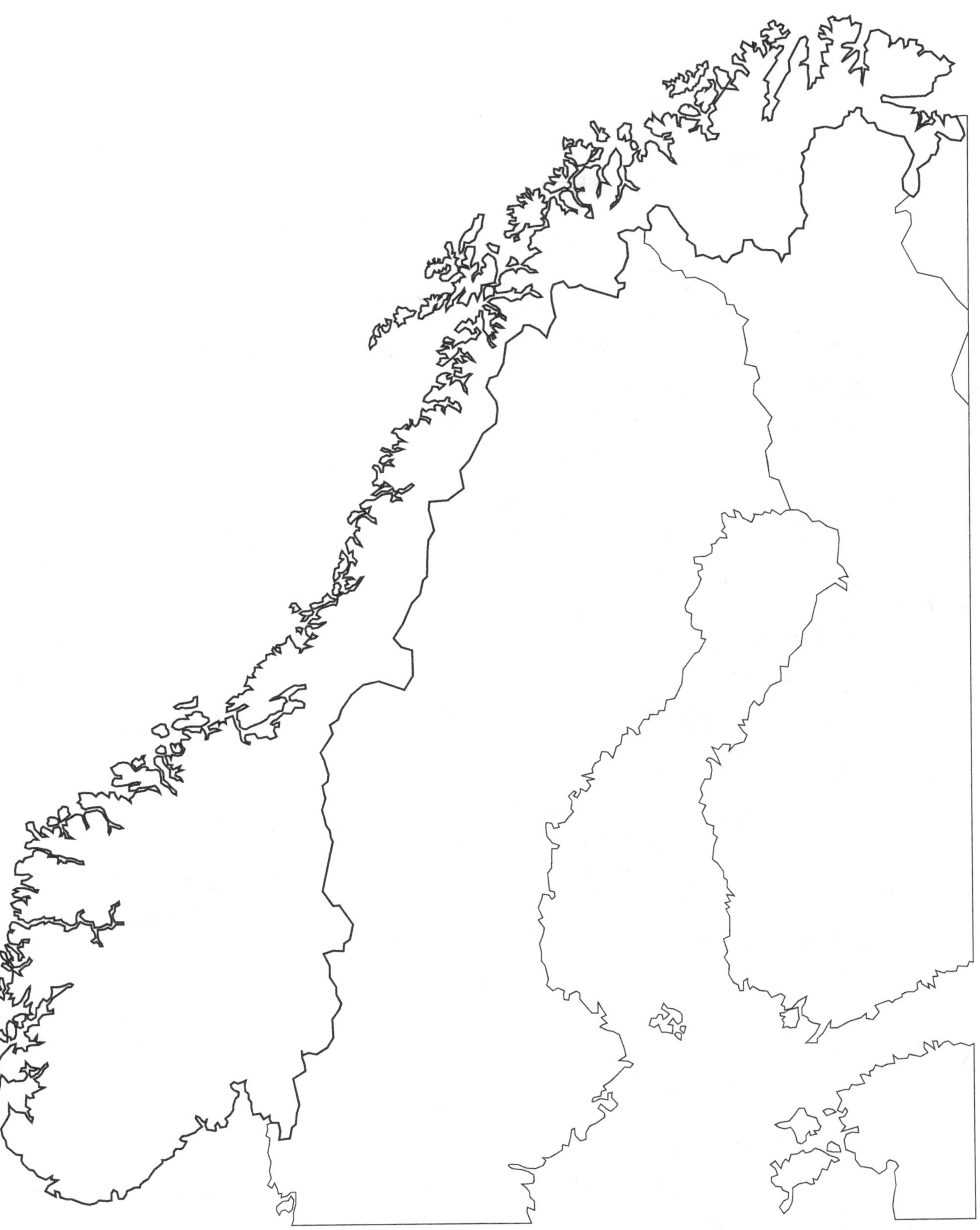

© Copyright Bruce Jones Design Inc. 2020
www.mapsfordesign.com

Poland

© Copyright Bruce Jones Design Inc. 2020
www.mapsfordesign.com

70

Poland

© Copyright Bruce Jones Design Inc. 2020
www.mapsfordesign.com

Portugal

© Copyright Bruce Jones Design Inc. 2020
www.mapsfordesign.com

Portugal

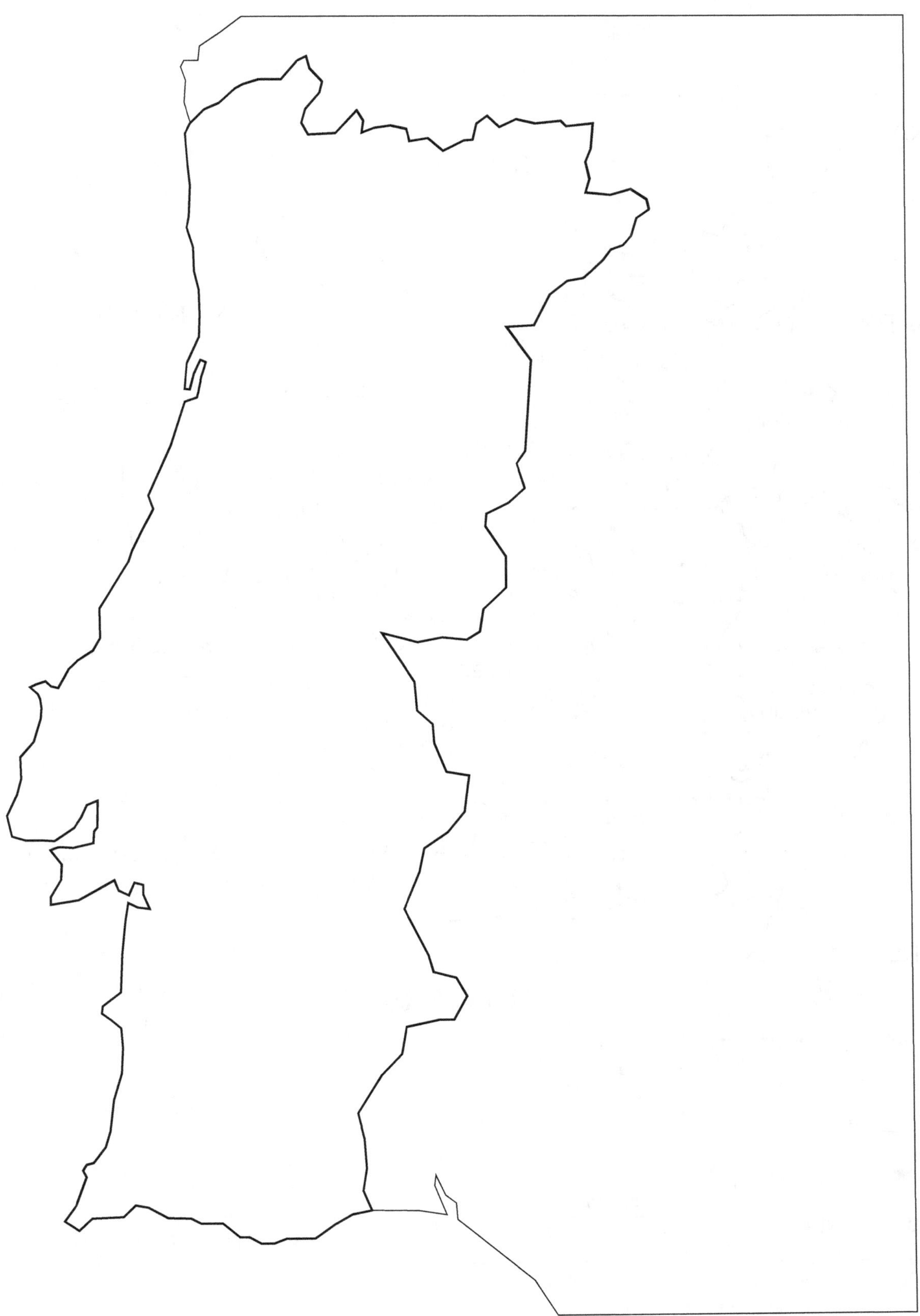

© Copyright Bruce Jones Design Inc. 2020
www.mapsfordesign.com

© Copyright Bruce Jones Design Inc. 2020
www.mapsfordesign.com

Romania

© Copyright Bruce Jones Design Inc. 2020
www.mapsfordesign.com

Russia

© Copyright Bruce Jones Design Inc. 2020
www.mapsfordesign.com

An oblast is named only when its name differs from that of its administrative center.
Moscow and St. Petersburg are federal cities having oblast-level status.

Russia

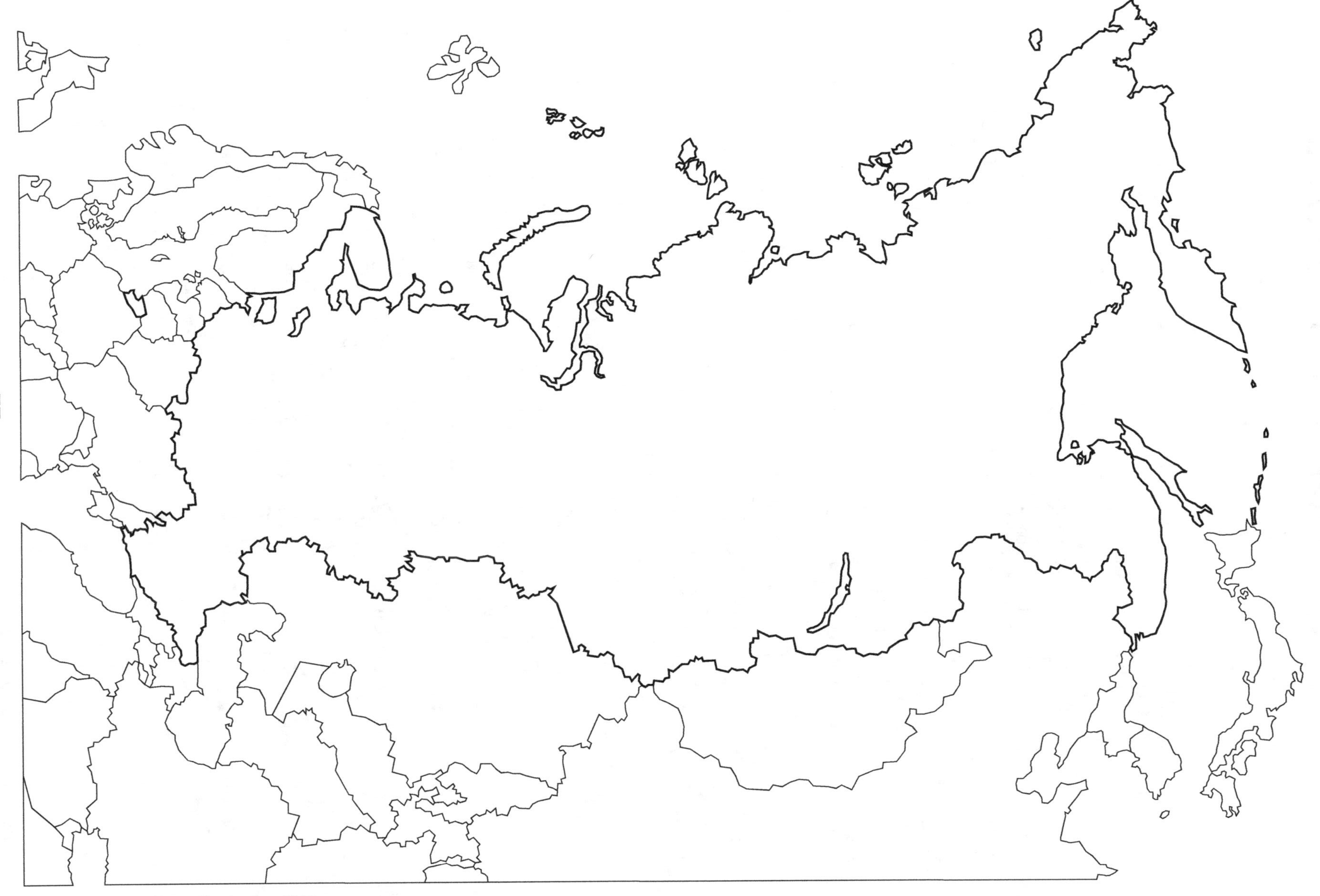

© Copyright Bruce Jones Design Inc. 2020
www.mapsfordesign.com

Serbia and Kosovo

© Copyright Bruce Jones Design Inc. 2020
www.mapsfordesign.com

78

Serbia and Kosovo

© Copyright Bruce Jones Design Inc. 2020
www.mapsfordesign.com

Slovakia

© Copyright Bruce Jones Design Inc. 2020
www.mapsfordesign.com

Slovakia

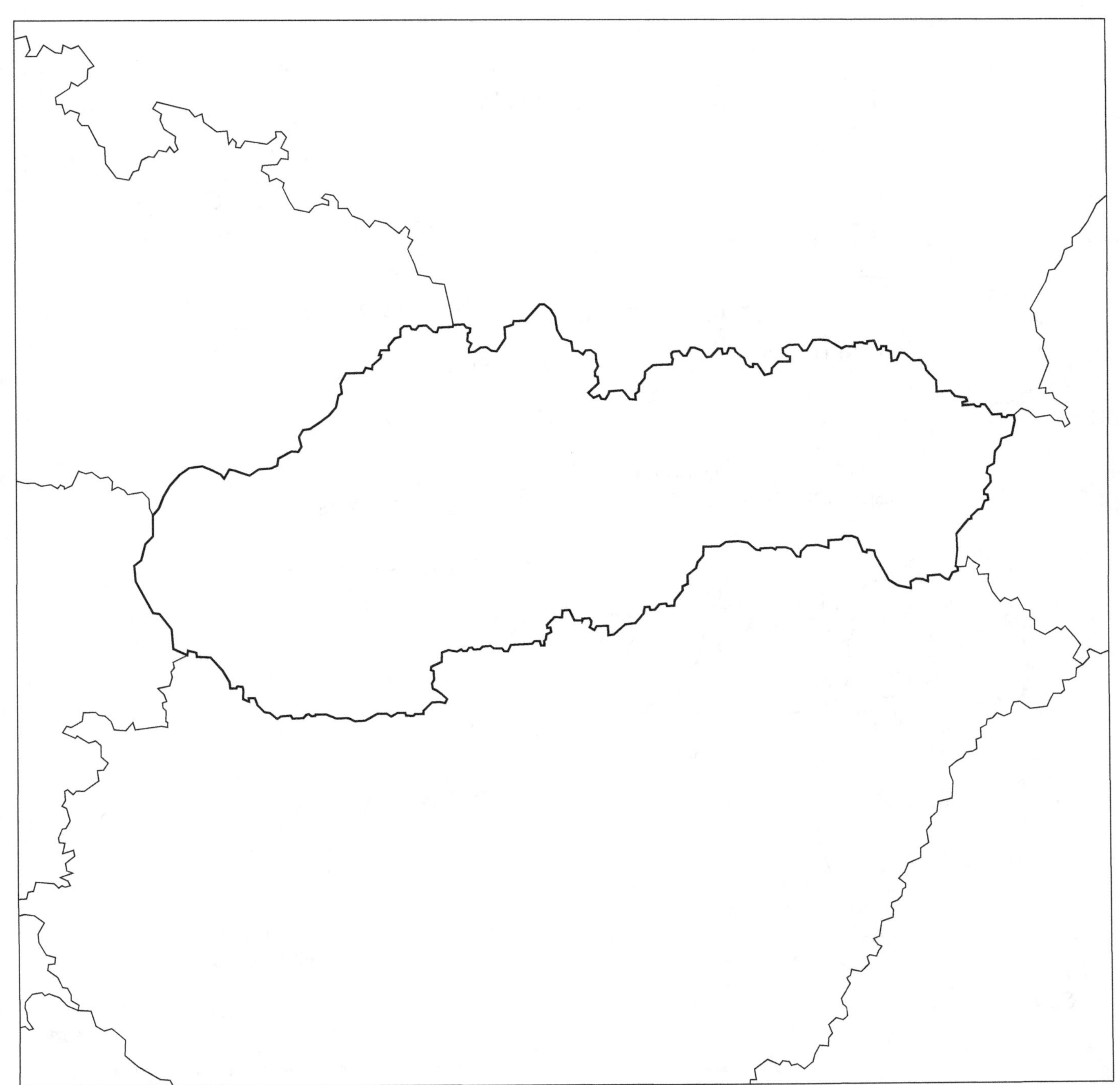

© Copyright Bruce Jones Design Inc. 2020
www.mapsfordesign.com

Slovenia

Administrative districts and capitals proposed but not finalized

© Copyright Bruce Jones Design Inc. 2020
www.mapsfordesign.com

Slovenia

© Copyright Bruce Jones Design Inc. 2020
www.mapsfordesign.com

Spain and Portugal
Provinces and Municipalities

© Copyright Bruce Jones Design Inc. 2020
www.mapsfordesign.com

Spain Autonomous Communities
Portugal Provinces

© Copyright Bruce Jones Design Inc. 2020
www.mapsfordesign.com

Spain
Autonomous Communities

© Copyright Bruce Jones Design Inc. 2020
www.mapsfordesign.com

Spain and Portugal

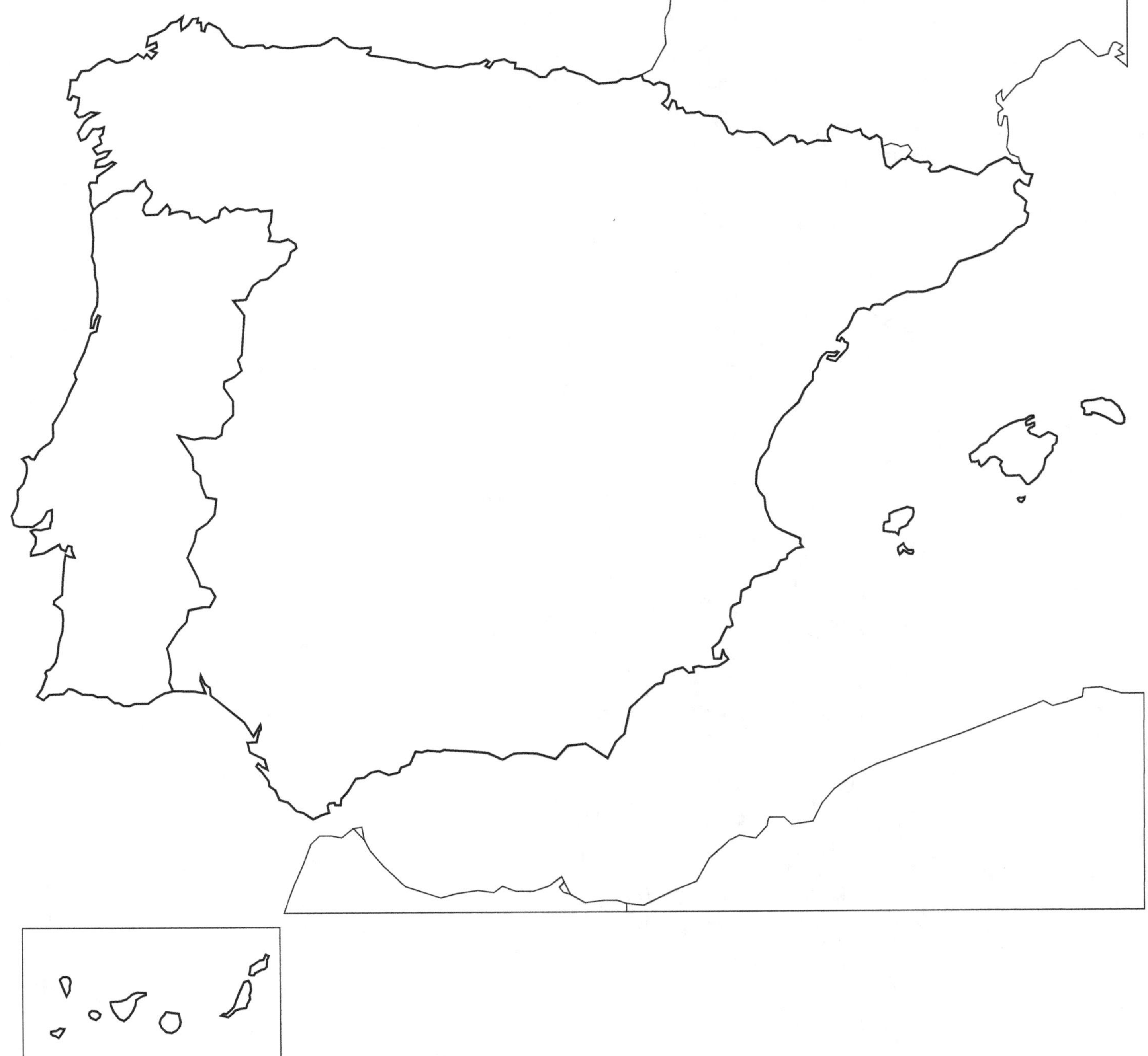

© Copyright Bruce Jones Design Inc. 2020
www.mapsfordesign.com

Sweden

© Copyright Bruce Jones Design Inc. 2020
www.mapsfordesign.com

Sweden

© Copyright Bruce Jones Design Inc. 2020
www.mapsfordesign.com

Switzerland

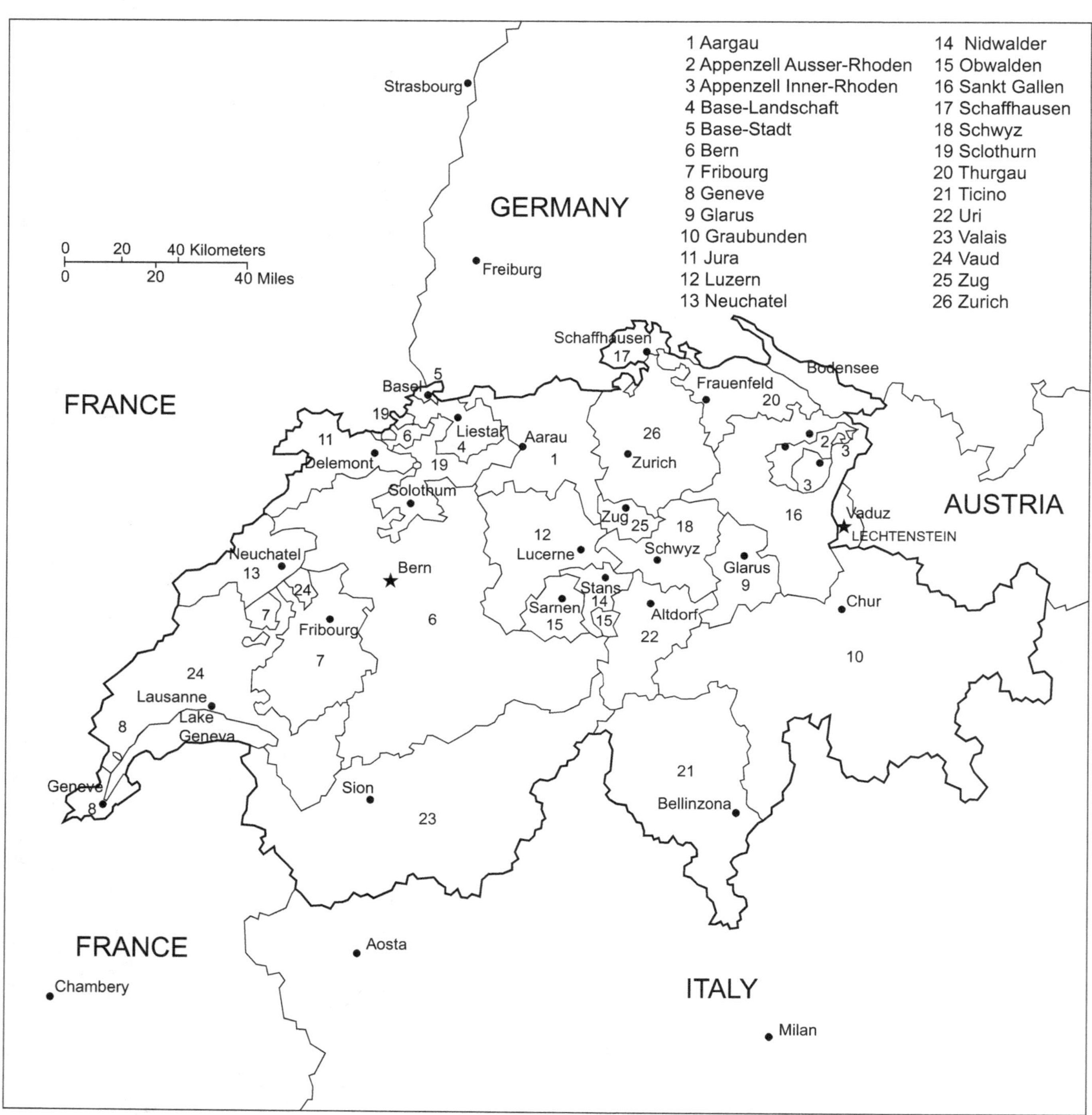

© Copyright Bruce Jones Design Inc. 2020
www.mapsfordesign.com

Switzerland

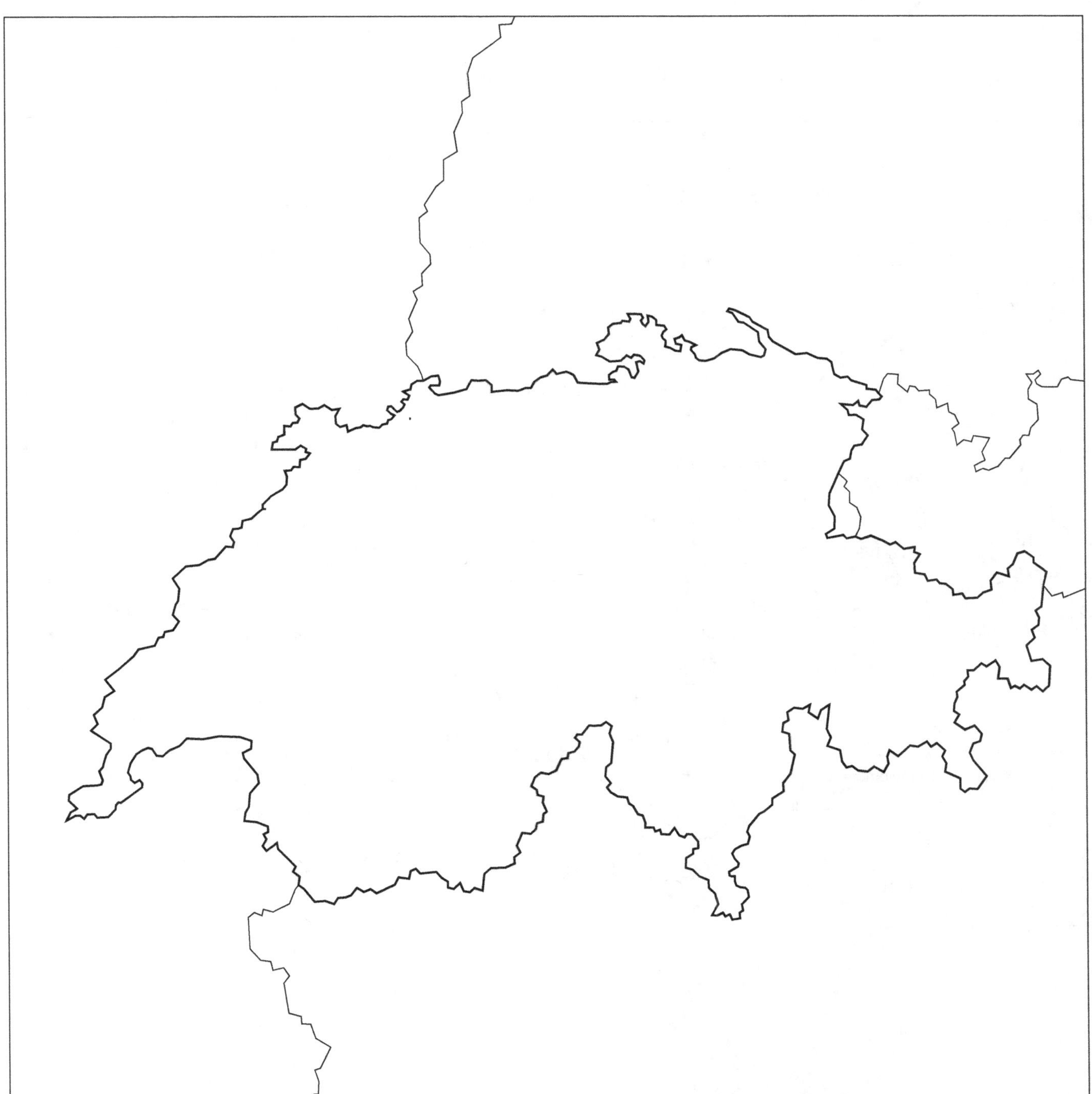

© Copyright Bruce Jones Design Inc. 2020
www.mapsfordesign.com

Ukraine

© Copyright Bruce Jones Design Inc. 2020
www.mapsfordesign.com

Ukraine

© Copyright Bruce Jones Design Inc. 2020
www.mapsfordesign.com

United Kingdom & Ireland

© Copyright Bruce Jones Design Inc. 2020
www.mapsfordesign.com

United Kingdom & Ireland

© Copyright Bruce Jones Design Inc. 2020
www.mapsfordesign.com

Liechtenstein and The Vatican

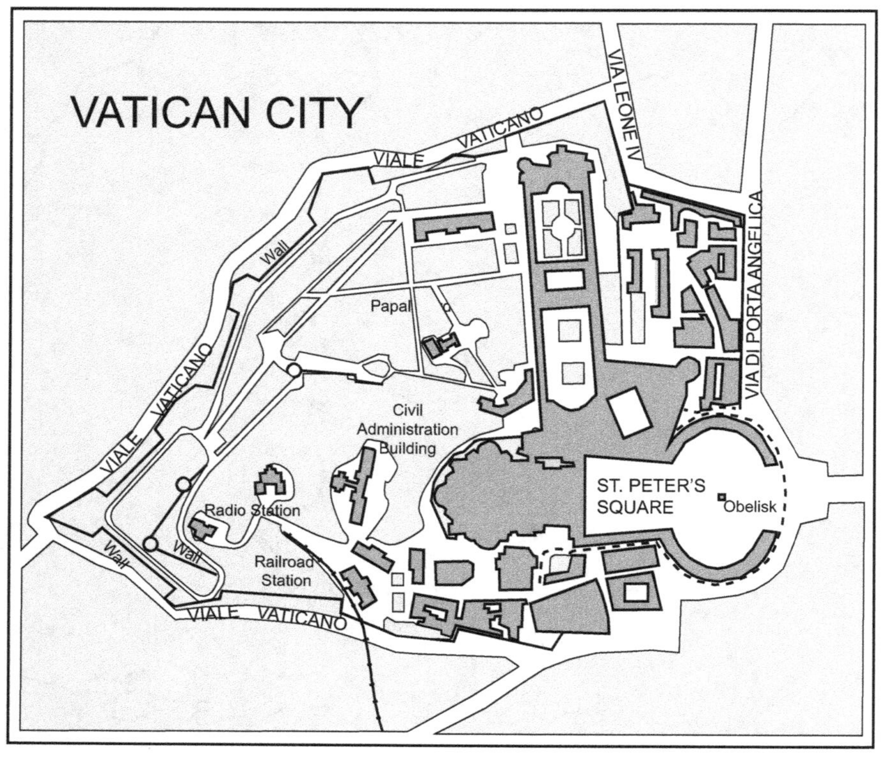

© Copyright Bruce Jones Design Inc. 2020
www.mapsfordesign.com

Liechtenstein and The Vatican

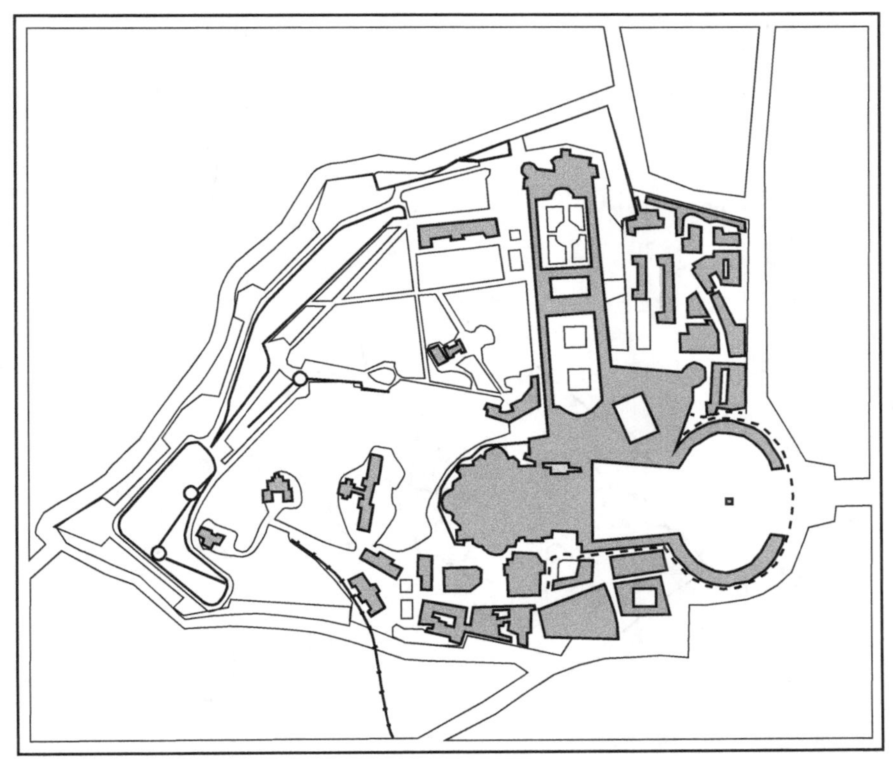

© Copyright Bruce Jones Design Inc. 2020
www.mapsfordesign.com

Andorra and Monaco

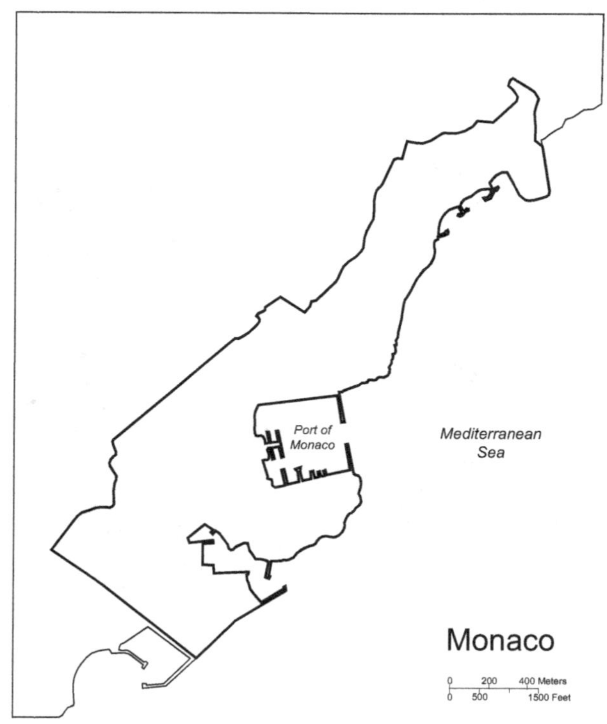

© Copyright Bruce Jones Design Inc. 2020
www.mapsfordesign.com

Andorra and Monaco

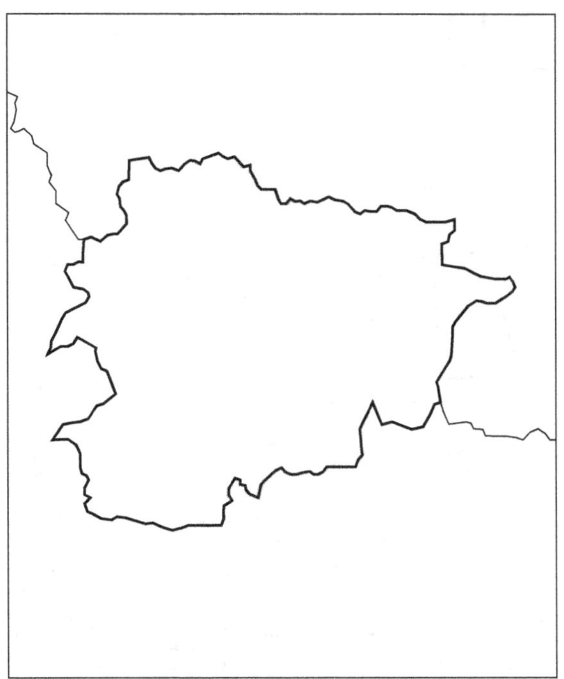

© Copyright Bruce Jones Design Inc. 2020
www.mapsfordesign.com

United States of America

© Copyright Bruce Jones Design Inc. 2020
www.mapsfordesign.com

United States of America

© Copyright Bruce Jones Design Inc. 2020
www.mapsfordesign.com

World Map — Mercator Projection

© Copyright Bruce Jones Design Inc. 2020
www.mapsfordesign.com

World Map — Mercator Projection

© Copyright Bruce Jones Design Inc. 2020
www.mapsfordesign.com

Check Out All Our Map Books

OK TO PHOTOCOPY
FOR SHARING

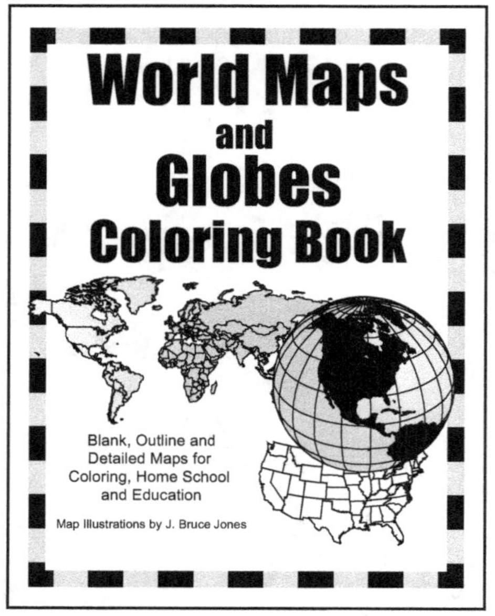

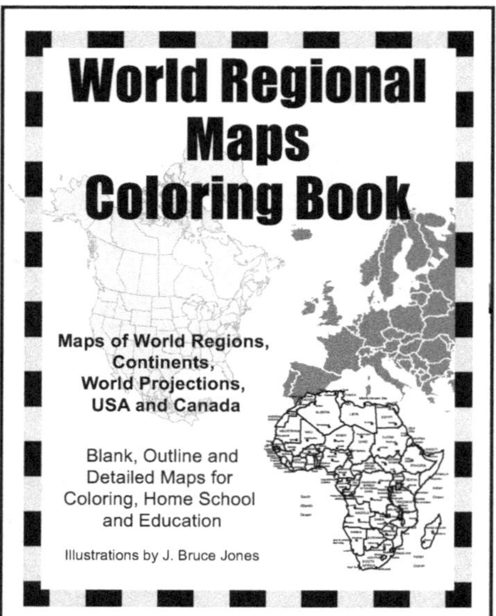

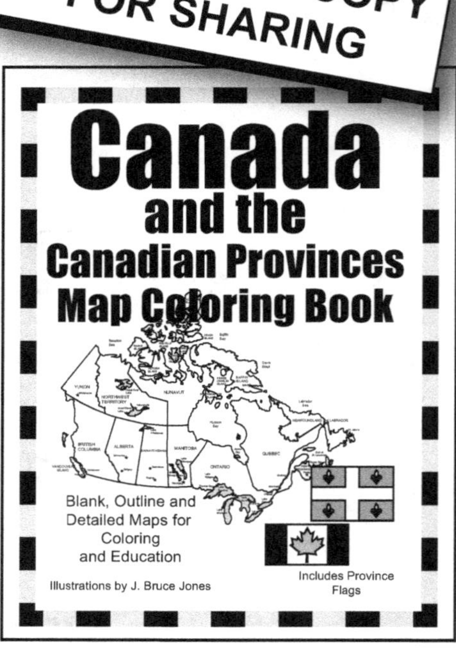

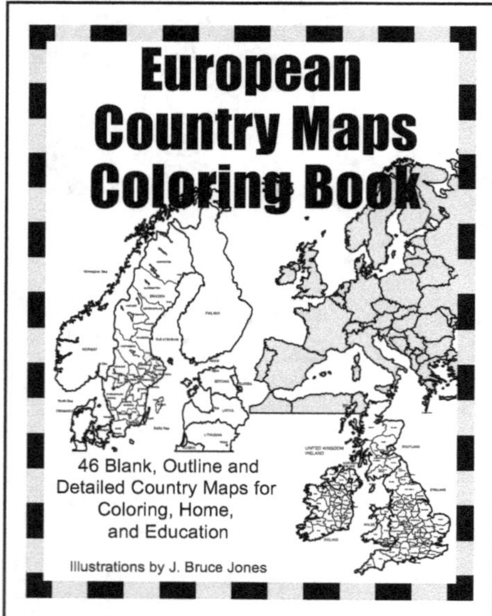

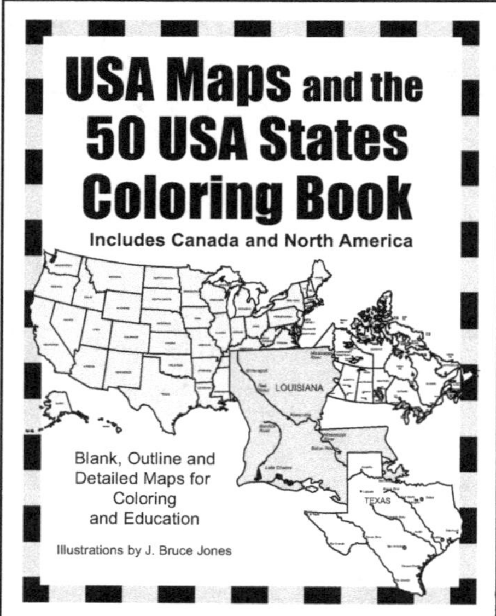

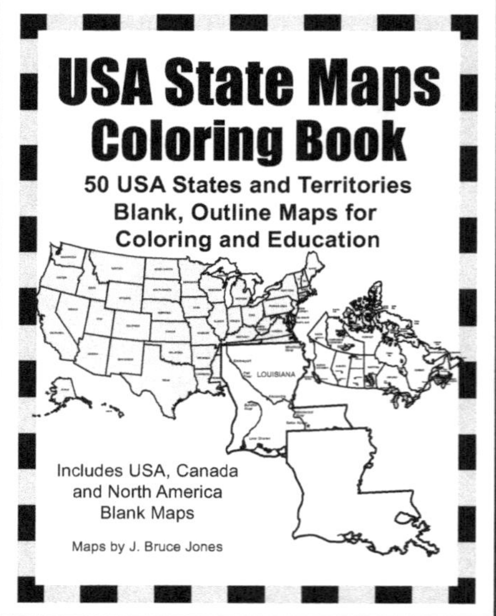

Blank, Outline and Detailed Maps for Coloring, Homeschool and Education

Blank, Outline, Printable PDF Map Sets and Editable Clip Art Maps

Perfect for Education, Home and School

Individual, Blank, Printable, Outline PDF Map Sets Your Students Can Trace and Color

- Learn geography, add names and features.

- Create lessons, games, in-class quizzes, study aids.

- Help your students learn the names and location of the states, countries, world regions and more.

- Students can trace the outlines of the blank maps, highlight continents and countries.

- Each map is an individual PDF file that can be printed out.

- USA, States, Canada, World Regions and Globes

- **A great teaching resource**

World of Maps Clip Art

Our Digital Map Collection includes all our easy to edit, royalty free, PowerPoint and Adobe Illustrator clip art maps. Plus a jpg version of every map.

- Editable Maps in PowerPoint and Adobe Illustrator

- PowerPoint maps also work in Keynote and Google Slides

- Have the entire collection at your finger tips.

Perfect for educational projects, teacher resources, scrapbooking, graphic design.

- Great for homeschool, education, or home decor images and posters.

- Each PowerPoint or Illustrator country, state or world map can be colored, and customized. Text can be edited or added.

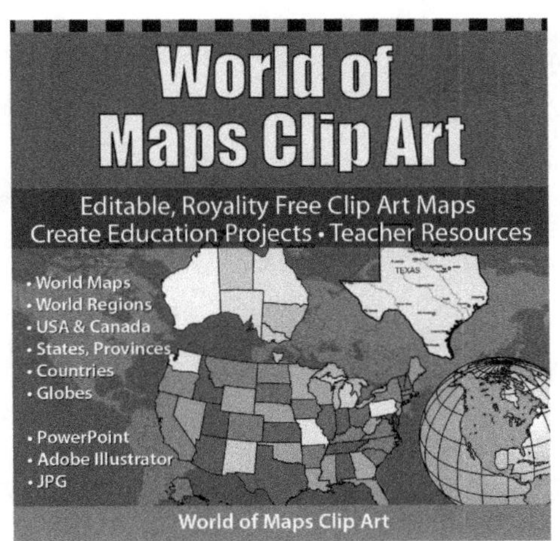

Visit www.FreeUSandWorldMaps.com

www.ingramcontent.com/pod-product-compliance
Lightning Source LLC
Chambersburg PA
CBHW081235250726
48654CB00012B/1334